# Save Our

# Giant Panda

Louise and Richard Spilsbury

Heinemann Library
Chicago, Illinois

© 2006 Heinemann Library
a division of Reed Elsevier Inc.
Chicago, Illinois

Customer Service   888–454–2279

Visit our website at www.heinemannlibrary.com

Photo research by Hannah Taylor and Fiona Orbell
Designed by Michelle Lisseter and Ron Kamen
Printed in China, by South China Printing Co. Ltd.

10 09 08 07 06
10 9 8 7 6 5 4 3 2 1

**Library of Congress Cataloging-in-Publication Data**
Spilsbury, Louise.
Save the giant panda / Louise and Richard Spilsbury.
    p. cm. -- (Save our animals!)
Includes bibliographical references and index.
ISBN-10: 1-4034-7807-4 (library binding-hardcover)   ISBN-10: 1-4034-7815-5 (pbk.)
  1.  Giant panda--Juvenile literature. 2.  Giant panda--Conservation
--Juvenile literature. I. Spilsbury, Richard, 1963- II. Title. III. Series.

QL737.C214S65 2006
599.789--dc22

2005027999

**Acknowledgments**
The author and publisher are grateful to the following for permission to reproduce copyright
material: Ardea pp. **4** top (Y A Betrand), **5** top left (J Rajput); Corbis pp. **22, 28** (K Su), **24**
(Reuters/ Brazil/ Stringer); Digital Vision pp. **5** middle, **11**; FLPA/Minden Pictures p. **10** (K Wothe);
Getty Images/China Photos pp. **19, 23, 26, 29**; Naturepl.com pp. **4** bottom left (M Carwardine),
**17** (S Flood); NHPA p. **7** (A Bannister); Oxford Scientific pp. **4** middle, **5** top right, **13, 14, 27**
(K Su); Photolibrary.com/Oxford Scientific pp. **6, 12**; Still Pictures pp. **5** bottom, **9, 21** (F Polking),
**15** (M Carwardine), **16** (Uniphoto Press), **18** (Zi Yi/UNEP); WWF p. **25**.

Cover photograph of giant panda, reproduced with permission of Corbis Sygma/ Bill Vaughn.

The publishers would like to thank staff at WWF Qinling Panda Focal Project for their assistance
in the preparation of this book.

Every effort has been made to contact copyright holders of any material reproduced in this
book. Any omissions will be rectified in subsequent printings if notice is given to the publisher.

**Disclaimer**
All Internet addresses (URLs) given in this book were valid at the time of going to press.
However, due to the dynamic nature of the Internet, some addresses may have changed or
ceased to exist since publication. While the author and the publishers regret any inconvenience
this may cause readers, no responsibility for any such changes can be accepted by either the
author or the publishers.

> Some words are shown in bold, **like this**. You can find out what they mean
> by looking in the glossary.

# Contents

# Animals in Trouble

There are many different types, or **species**, of animals. Some species are in danger of becoming **extinct**. This means that all the animals from that species might die.

All the animals shown here are in danger of becoming extinct. These species need to be saved. The giant panda is one of them.

# The Giant Panda

Giant pandas are very easy to recognize. They are large, fluffy bears with black and white hair. Their legs, shoulders, ears, and eye patches are black.

A giant panda has ovals of black hair around its eyes.

*Pandas use their sharp claws to help them climb trees.*

Giant pandas mainly stay on the ground and walk on their four legs. They can climb trees to sleep or to look around. They grip things with their claws.

# Where Can You Find Giant Pandas?

In the past, giant pandas lived all over southern and eastern China. They also lived in Myanmar and Vietnam. Today they only live in a few parts of southwest China.

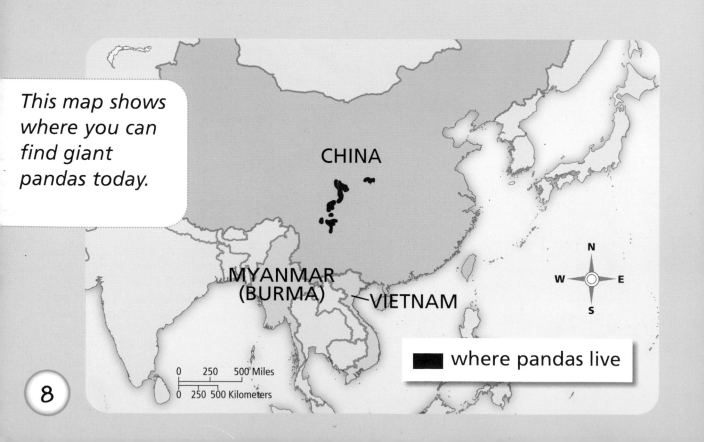

This map shows where you can find giant pandas today.

CHINA

MYANMAR (BURMA)

VIETNAM

N
W • E
S

0    250    500 Miles
0  250 500 Kilometers

■ where pandas live

*Giant pandas live on mountain slopes, like these.*

Giant pandas live in forests on high mountain slopes. It is cold and rainy there. The giant panda's thick, woolly fur keeps it warm and dry.

# What Do Giant Pandas Eat?

Giant pandas only eat **bamboo**.
Bamboo is a type of giant grass plant.
Giant pandas eat the **shoots**, stems,
and leaves of bamboo plants.

*The giant panda has five short fingers and a long wristbone.*

Giant pandas have to eat a lot of bamboo to stay healthy. They spend about 16 hours of every day eating.

Giant pandas usually sit down to eat. They hold food in their front paws.

# Young Giant Pandas

Baby pandas are called **cubs**. They are usually born in a cave. They stay there for six weeks. Pandas are **mammals**, so cubs drink milk from their mothers.

This panda cub is about four weeks old.

*A panda cub starts following its mother when it is three months old.*

A cub starts to eat **bamboo** when it is four months old. It stays with its mother for two years. After that the panda will live alone.

# Natural Dangers

Adult giant pandas are not in danger from other animals. They are too big and strong to be attacked. Snow leopards sometimes catch panda **cubs**.

*Snow leopards eat giant panda cubs if they catch them.*

If the weather is too cold, or the plants get a disease, the **bamboo** dies. When this happens, giant pandas can die because they have no food.

If there is no bamboo, giant pandas have nothing to eat.

# Hunting and Trapping

In the past, people trapped and killed giant pandas for their fur and meat. Now it is against the law to kill pandas, but some hunters still do.

*This policeman has taken a panda skin away from a hunter.*

*This man has found a trap that could harm giant pandas.*

Some pandas are hurt by accident. Hunters put down traps to catch other animals, such as deer. Giant pandas get badly injured if they step on the traps.

# Dangers to the Giant Panda's World

Trees in China's mountain forests are being cut down. People are selling the wood and building towns on the land.

*Destroying the forests means less food and less space for pandas.*

Once a year, **male** pandas search for a **female** to **mate** with. If there are towns in the way, pandas cannot find each other easily. Fewer **cubs** are born.

*These people are helping a giant panda in a tree.*

# How Many Giant Pandas Are There?

There are about 1,600 giant pandas in the wild today. They all live alone. Most live in small areas with fewer than 20 other pandas living nearby.

**Year**

1980s

2004

*The number of pandas is slowly growing, but there are still not many of them.*

 = 500

There are more people in China today than ever before. They use more wood and take more land to live on.

We need to protect the giant pandas' **habitat** to save them.

# How Are Giant Pandas Being Saved?

China has made more than 50 **reserves** for giant pandas. Reserves are areas of land where wild animals, such as giant pandas, can live in safety.

In reserves people are not allowed to cut down trees.

Some reserves have **breeding centers**, such as this one.

In China it is against the law to hunt giant pandas. People called **wardens** protect the giant pandas in their reserve and keep hunters out.

# Who Is Helping Giant Pandas?

**WWF** is a **charity** that helps pandas. It is showing people in China how to raise money to protect them. Today tourists pay to watch the pandas.

The giant panda is the symbol of WWF.

*Wardens look carefully to find out where giant pandas live.*

In the Qinling (you say "Chinling") Mountains, there are 12 new panda **reserves**. The pandas can move safely from one reserve to another.

# How Can You Help?

It is important to know that giant pandas are in danger. Then you can learn how to help to save them. Read, watch, and find out all you can about giant pandas.

*It is important to learn how to help save pandas, so that they will not become **extinct**.*

Here are some things you can do
to help.

- Join a group, such as **WWF**, that raises
  money for giant panda projects.
- Visit zoos where giant pandas live.
  Some zoos raise money to help wild
  giant pandas.

# The Future for Giant Pandas

Giant pandas may soon become **extinct**. In China about half of all pandas live in **reserves**. More pandas will be saved if their **habitat** is protected.

Giant pandas could become extinct if we do not protect their habitat.

Giant pandas are having **cubs** in safe **breeding centers** in China. Some of these pandas will be set free, into the wild. Then there will be more pandas.

*Breeding centers give pandas a safe place to have their babies.*

# Giant Panda Facts

- Giant pandas live for about 25 years in the wild.
- A newborn panda **cub** is only as long as a pencil.
- When giant panda cubs are born, they are pink and have no hair.
- Giant pandas are good climbers. They are also good swimmers.

# Find Out More

Eckart, Edana. *Giant Panda*. Danbury, CT: Children's Press, 2003.

Gibbons, Gail. *Giant Pandas*. New York: Holiday House, 2004.

# Web Sites

To find out more about **WWF**, visit their Web site:

www.worldwildlife.org

# Glossary

**bamboo**   tall plant with green leaves. Pandas eat only bamboo.

**breeding center**   safe place where male and female animals can mate and have babies

**charity**   group that collects money to help animals or people in need

**cub**   baby panda

**extinct**   when all the animals in a species die out and the species no longer exists

**female**   animal that can become a mother when it grows up. Women and girls are female people.

**habitat**   place where plants and animals grow and live. A forest is a kind of habitat.

**mammal**   animal that feeds its babies with the mother's milk and has some hair on its body

**male**   animal that can become a father when it grows up. Men and boys are male people.

**mate**   what male and female animals do to make babies

**reserve**   area of land where animals are protected and the habitat is looked after

**shoot**   beginning of a new plant

**species**   group of animals that can have babies together

**warden**   person who guards reserves

**WWF**   charity that helps endangered species. It is also called the World Wildlife Fund.

# Index